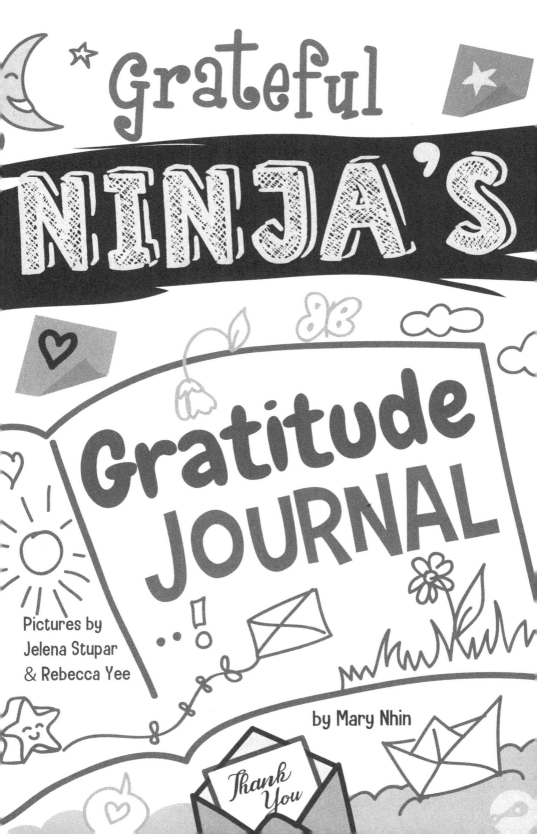

Email us at
growgritpress@gmail.com
to get FREE extras!

This book is dedicated to my children— Mikey, Kobe, and Jojo.
Journaling is like having a friend that never gives up on you.

This Journal Belongs to:

My Gratitude Journal Partner is:

S M T W TH F S Date __/__/__

I'm Thankful For:

1. _____

2. _____

3. _____

I was happy when I spent time with:

I feel:

What was awesome about your day today?
Write or draw about it below:

S M T W TH F S Date __/__/__

I'm Thankful For:

1. _____

2. _____

3. _____

I was happy when I spent time with:

I feel:

What was awesome about your day today? Write or draw about it below:

S M T W TH F S Date __/__/__

I'm Thankful For:

1. _____
2. _____
3. _____

I was happy when I spent time with:

I feel:

What was awesome about your day today? Write or draw about it below:

S M T W TH F S Date __/__/__

I'm Thankful For:

1. _____

2. _____

3. _____

I was happy when I spent time with:

I feel:

What was awesome about your day today? Write or draw about it below:

S M T W TH F S Date __/__/__

I'm Thankful For:

1. _____

2. _____

3. _____

I was happy when I
spent time with:

I feel:

What was awesome about your day today?
Write or draw about it below:

Gift Yourself a Gratitude Jar

Find and decorate an empty jar. Think about people, things, and places you are grateful for. Write them down to place in your gratitide jar!

S M T W TH F S Date __/__/__

I'm Thankful For:

1. _____

2. _____

3. _____

I was happy when I spent time with:

I feel:

What was awesome about your day today? Write or draw about it below:

S M T W TH F S Date __/__/__

I'm Thankful For:

1. _____

2. _____

3. _____

I was happy when I spent time with:

I feel:

What was awesome about your day today? Write or draw about it below:

S M T W TH F S Date __/__/__

I'm Thankful For:

1. _____

2. _____

3. _____

I was happy when I
spent time with:

I feel:

What was awesome about your day today?
Write or draw about it below:

S M T W TH F S Date __/__/__

I'm Thankful For:

1. _____

2. _____

3. _____

I was happy when I spent time with:

I feel:

What was awesome about your day today? Write or draw about it below:

S M T W TH F S Date __/__/__

I'm Thankful For:

1. _____
2. _____
3. _____

I was happy when I spent time with:

I feel:

What was awesome about your day today? Write or draw about it below:

I am Grateful

S M T W TH F S Date __/__/__

I'm Thankful For:

1. _____

2. _____

3. _____

I was happy when I spent time with:

I feel:

What was awesome about your day today? Write or draw about it below:

S M T W TH F S Date __/__/__

I'm Thankful For:

1. _____

2. _____

3. _____

**I was happy when I
spent time with:**

I feel:

What was awesome about your day today?
Write or draw about it below:

S M T W TH F S Date __/__/__

I'm Thankful For:

1. _____
2. _____
3. _____

I was happy when I spent time with:

I feel:

What was awesome about your day today? Write or draw about it below:

S M T W TH F S Date __ / __ / __

I'm Thankful For:

1. _____

2. _____

3. _____

I was happy when I spent time with:

I feel:

What was awesome about your day today?
Write or draw about it below:

S M T W TH F S Date __ / __ / __

I'm Thankful For:

1. _____

2. _____

3. _____

I was happy when I spent time with:

I feel:

What was awesome about your day today? Write or draw about it below:

Give Gratitude Everyday!

Take some time to think of things you are grateful for everyday before dinner time or at before bedtime.

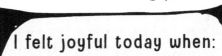

Today I am grateful for:

I felt joyful today when:

The best part of my day was:

I can make tomorrow a great day by:

S M T W TH F S Date __/__/__

I'm Thankful For:

1. _____

2. _____

3. _____

I was happy when I spent time with:

I feel:

What was awesome about your day today?
Write or draw about it below:

S M T W TH F S Date __/__/__

I'm Thankful For:

1. _____

2. _____

3. _____

I was happy when I spent time with:

I feel:

What was awesome about your day today? Write or draw about it below:

S M T W TH F S Date __/__/__

I'm Thankful For:

1. _____

2. _____

3. _____

I was happy when I
spent time with:

I feel:

What was awesome about your day today?
Write or draw about it below:

S M T W TH F S Date __/__/__

I'm Thankful For:

1. _____

2. _____

3. _____

I was happy when I spent time with:

I feel:

What was awesome about your day today?
Write or draw about it below:

S M T W TH F S Date __/__/__

I'm Thankful For:

1. _____

2. _____

3. _____

I was happy when I
spent time with:

I feel:

What was awesome about your day today?
Write or draw about it below:

I am Thankful for My Family

Draw and color in a picture of your family.

S M T W TH F S Date __/__/__

I'm Thankful For:

1. _____

2. _____

3. _____

I was happy when I spent time with:

I feel:

What was awesome about your day today? Write or draw about it below:

S M T W TH F S Date __/__/__

I'm Thankful For:

1. _____

2. _____

3. _____

I was happy when I spent time with:

I feel:

What was awesome about your day today?
Write or draw about it below:

S M T W TH F S Date __/__/__

I'm Thankful For:

1. _____

2. _____

3. _____

I was happy when I
spent time with:

I feel:

What was awesome about your day today?
Write or draw about it below:

S M T W TH F S Date __/__/__

I'm Thankful For:

1. _____

2. _____

3. _____

I was happy when I spent time with:

I feel:

What was awesome about your day today? Write or draw about it below:

S M T W TH F S Date __/__/__

I'm Thankful For:

1. _____

2. _____

3. _____

I was happy when I spent time with:

I feel:

What was awesome about your day today? Write or draw about it below:

Grow Our Thank You's
and Please's

Think about someone who did something nice, generous, or kind for you recently. Write them a Thank You Letter in the space below. Tell them why you are saying thank you. When you are done, you can cut out the letter and mail it to that person! Imagine how happy they will be!

Dear _____ ,

Thank you for

_____

_____

_____

_____

_____

_____

_____

From_____

S M T W TH F S Date __/__/__

I'm Thankful For:

1. _____

2. _____

3. _____

I was happy when I spent time with:

I feel:

What was awesome about your day today? Write or draw about it below:

S M T W TH F S Date __/__/__

I'm Thankful For:

1. _____

2. _____

3. _____

I was happy when I spent time with:

I feel:

What was awesome about your day today? Write or draw about it below:

S M T W TH F S Date __/__/__

I'm Thankful For:

1. _____

2. _____

3. _____

I was happy when I spent time with:

I feel:

What was awesome about your day today? Write or draw about it below:

S M T W TH F S Date __/__/__

I'm Thankful For:

1. _____

2. _____

3. _____

I was happy when I
spent time with:

I feel:

What was awesome about your day today?
Write or draw about it below:

S M T W TH F S Date __/__/__

I'm Thankful For:

1. _____

2. _____

3. _____

I was happy when I spent time with:

I feel:

What was awesome about your day today? Write or draw about it below:

I am Grateful for my Health

S M T W TH F S Date __/__/__

I'm Thankful For:

1. _____

2. _____

3. _____

I was happy when I spent time with:

I feel:

What was awesome about your day today? Write or draw about it below:

S M T W TH F S Date __/__/__

I'm Thankful For:

1. _____

2. _____

3. _____

I was happy when I spent time with:

I feel:

What was awesome about your day today? Write or draw about it below:

S M T W TH F S Date __/__/__

I'm Thankful For:

1. _____

2. _____

3. _____

I was happy when I spent time with:

I feel:

What was awesome about your day today? Write or draw about it below:

S M T W TH F S Date __/__/__

I'm Thankful For:

1. _____

2. _____

3. _____

I was happy when I
spent time with:

I feel:

What was awesome about your day today?
Write or draw about it below:

S M T W TH F S Date __/__/__

I'm Thankful For:

1. _____

2. _____

3. _____

I was happy when I spent time with:

I feel:

What was awesome about your day today? Write or draw about it below:

My Gratitude List

Write down things you are grateful for next to each word.

Book _____

Song _____

Movie _____

Person _____

Animal _____

Smell _____

Food _____

Drink _____

Color _____

Season _____

Holiday _____

Place _____

S M T W TH F S Date __/__/__

I'm Thankful For:

1. _____

2. _____

3. _____

I was happy when I spent time with:

I feel:

What was awesome about your day today? Write or draw about it below:

S M T W TH F S Date __/__/__

I'm Thankful For:

1. _____

2. _____

3. _____

I was happy when I spent time with:

I feel:

What was awesome about your day today? Write or draw about it below:

S M T W TH F S Date __/__/__

I'm Thankful For:

1. _____

2. _____

3. _____

I was happy when I spent time with:

I feel:

What was awesome about your day today? Write or draw about it below:

S M T W TH F S Date __/__/__

I'm Thankful For:

1. _____

2. _____

3. _____

I was happy when I
spent time with:

I feel:

What was awesome about your day today?
Write or draw about it below:

S M T W TH F S Date __/__/__

I'm Thankful For:

1. _____

2. _____

3. _____

I was happy when I spent time with:

I feel:

What was awesome about your day today? Write or draw about it below:

I am Thankful for Peace in the World.

S M T W TH F S Date __/__/__

I'm Thankful For:

1. _____

2. _____

3. _____

I was happy when I spent time with:

I feel:

What was awesome about your day today? Write or draw about it below:

S M T W TH F S Date __/__/__

I'm Thankful For:

1. _____

2. _____

3. _____

I was happy when I spent time with:

I feel:

What was awesome about your day today? Write or draw about it below:

S M T W TH F S Date __/__/__

I'm Thankful For:

1. _____

2. _____

3. _____

I was happy when I spent time with:

I feel:

What was awesome about your day today? Write or draw about it below:

S M T W TH F S Date __/__/__

I'm Thankful For:

1. _____

2. _____

3. _____

I was happy when I spent time with:

I feel:

What was awesome about your day today?
Write or draw about it below:

S M T W TH F S Date __/__/__

I'm Thankful For:

1. _____

2. _____

3. _____

I was happy when I
spent time with:

I feel:

What was awesome about your day today?
Write or draw about it below:

Give Thanks

Think of someone you know such as a family member, a friend, or a teacher. Think about why you are thankful for this person. Write a letter to them by filling in the empty spaces below.

Dear _____,

Thank you for being a great

_____.

My favorite part about you is

_____.

I am thankful you taught me how

to _____.

I love when we _____

together.

You are great because

_____.

Love, _____

S M T W TH F S Date __/__/__

I'm Thankful For:

1. _____
2. _____
3. _____

I was happy when I spent time with:

I feel:

What was awesome about your day today? Write or draw about it below:

S M T W TH F S Date __/__/__

I'm Thankful For:

1. _____

2. _____

3. _____

**I was happy when I
spent time with:**

I feel:

**What was awesome about your day today?
Write or draw about it below:**

S M T W TH F S Date __/__/__

I'm Thankful For:

1. _____

2. _____

3. _____

I was happy when I spent time with:

I feel:

What was awesome about your day today?
Write or draw about it below:

S M T W TH F S Date __/__/__

I'm Thankful For:

1. _____

2. _____

3. _____

I was happy when I
spent time with:

I feel:

What was awesome about your day today?
Write or draw about it below:

S M T W TH F S Date __/__/__

I'm Thankful For:

1. _____

2. _____

3. _____

I was happy when I
spent time with:

I feel:

What was awesome about your day today?
Write or draw about it below:

I am Thankful for...

Draw and color in something you are thankful for.

S M T W TH F S Date __/__/__

I'm Thankful For:

1. _____

2. _____

3. _____

I was happy when I spent time with:

I feel:

What was awesome about your day today? Write or draw about it below:

S M T W TH F S Date __/__/__

I'm Thankful For:

1. _____

2. _____

3. _____

I was happy when I spent time with:

I feel:

What was awesome about your day today?
Write or draw about it below:

S M T W TH F S Date __/__/__

I'm Thankful For:

1. _____

2. _____

3. _____

I was happy when I
spent time with:

I feel:

What was awesome about your day today?
Write or draw about it below:

S M T W TH F S Date __/__/__

I'm Thankful For:

1. _____

2. _____

3. _____

I was happy when I
spent time with:

I feel:

What was awesome about your day today?
Write or draw about it below:

S M T W TH F S Date __/__/__

I'm Thankful For:

1. _____

2. _____

3. _____

I was happy when I spent time with:

I feel:

What was awesome about your day today? Write or draw about it below:

Mini Thank You Notes

Write a mini thank you note to someone in your life. When you're done, you can cut them out and share them! Think of the smiles this will bring to someone's face.

Dear _____,
Thank you for _____
_____
_____
From, _____
Thank You!

Dear _____,
Thank you for _____
_____
_____
From, _____
Thank You!

Dear _____,
Thank you for _____
_____
_____
From, _____
Thank You!

Dear _____,
Thank you for _____
_____
_____
From, _____
Thank You!

S M T W TH F S Date __/__/__

I'm Thankful For:

1. _____
2. _____
3. _____

I was happy when I spent time with:

I feel:

What was awesome about your day today? Write or draw about it below:

S M T W TH F S Date __/__/__

I'm Thankful For:

1. _____

2. _____

3. _____

I was happy when I
spent time with:

I feel:

What was awesome about your day today?
Write or draw about it below:

S M T W TH F S Date __/__/__

I'm Thankful For:

1. _____

2. _____

3. _____

I was happy when I
spent time with:

I feel:

What was awesome about your day today?
Write or draw about it below:

S M T W TH F S Date __/__/__

I'm Thankful For:

1. _____

2. _____

3. _____

I was happy when I spent time with:

I feel:

What was awesome about your day today?
Write or draw about it below:

S M T W TH F S Date __/__/__

I'm Thankful For:

1. _____

2. _____

3. _____

I was happy when I spent time with:

I feel:

What was awesome about your day today? Write or draw about it below:

I am Thankful for My Home

List or draw something you are thankful for in your home.

S M T W TH F S Date __ / __ / __

I'm Thankful For:

1. _____

2. _____

3. _____

I was happy when I spent time with:

I feel:

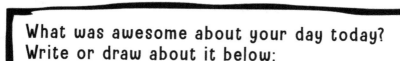

What was awesome about your day today? Write or draw about it below:

S M T W TH F S Date __/__/__

I'm Thankful For:

1. _____

2. _____

3. _____

I was happy when I spent time with:

I feel:

What was awesome about your day today? Write or draw about it below:

S M T W TH F S Date __/__/__

I'm Thankful For:

1. _____

2. _____

3. _____

I was happy when I spent time with:

I feel:

What was awesome about your day today? Write or draw about it below:

S M T W TH F S Date __/__/__

I'm Thankful For:

1. _____
2. _____
3. _____

I was happy when I spent time with:

I feel:

What was awesome about your day today? Write or draw about it below:

S M T W TH F S Date __/__/__

I'm Thankful For:

1. _____

2. _____

3. _____

I was happy when I spent time with:

I feel:

What was awesome about your day today? Write or draw about it below:

Grateful to be Me

I am grateful that I can:

What have you done that made you feel proud?

Write 3 things about yourself that you are grateful for:

1. _____

_____

2. _____

_____

3. _____

_____

S M T W TH F S Date __/__/__

I'm Thankful For:

1. _____

2. _____

3. _____

I was happy when I
spent time with:

I feel:

What was awesome about your day today?
Write or draw about it below:

S M T W TH F S Date __/__/__

I'm Thankful For:

1. _____

2. _____

3. _____

I was happy when I spent time with:

I feel:

What was awesome about your day today? Write or draw about it below:

S M T W TH F S Date __/__/__

I'm Thankful For:

1. _____

2. _____

3. _____

I was happy when I spent time with:

I feel:

What was awesome about your day today? Write or draw about it below:

S M T W TH F S Date __/__/__

I'm Thankful For:

1. _____

2. _____

3. _____

I was happy when I
spent time with:

I feel:

What was awesome about your day today?
Write or draw about it below:

S M T W TH F S Date __/__/__

I'm Thankful For:

1. _____
2. _____
3. _____

I was happy when I
spent time with:

I feel:

What was awesome about your day today?
Write or draw about it below:

I am Thankful for the Food I Eat.

S M T W TH F S Date __/__/__

I'm Thankful For:

1. _____

2. _____

3. _____

I was happy when I spent time with:

I feel:

What was awesome about your day today?
Write or draw about it below:

S M T W TH F S Date __/__/__

I'm Thankful For:

1. _____

2. _____

3. _____

I was happy when I spent time with:

I feel:

What was awesome about your day today? Write or draw about it below:

S M T W TH F S Date __/__/__

I'm Thankful For:

1. _____
2. _____
3. _____

I was happy when I spent time with:

I feel:

What was awesome about your day today? Write or draw about it below:

S M T W TH F S Date __/__/__

I'm Thankful For:

1. _____

2. _____

3. _____

I was happy when I spent time with:

I feel:

What was awesome about your day today?
Write or draw about it below:

S M T W TH F S Date __/__/__

I'm Thankful For:

1. _____

2. _____

3. _____

I was happy when I
spent time with:

I feel:

What was awesome about your day today?
Write or draw about it below:

Three Compliments

Give 3 compliments today to 3 different people. Write down each person's name and your compliment below.

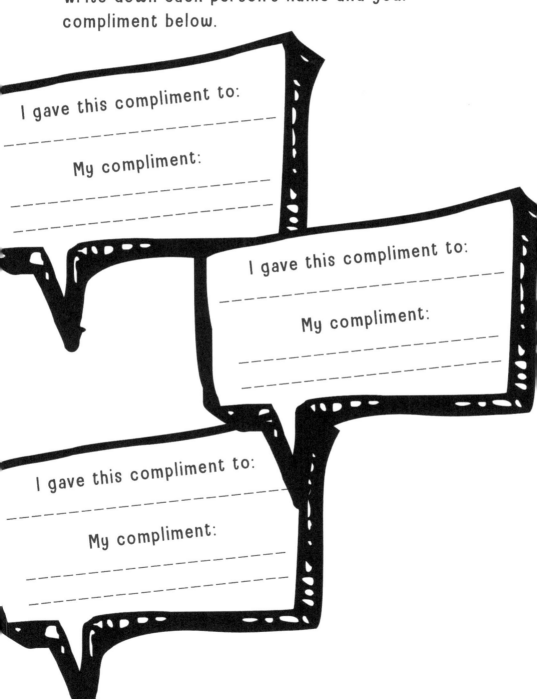

I gave this compliment to:
_____

My compliment:
_____

I gave this compliment to:
_____

My compliment:
_____

I gave this compliment to:
_____

My compliment:
_____

S M T W TH F S Date __/__/__

I'm Thankful For:

1. _____

2. _____

3. _____

I was happy when I spent time with:

I feel:

What was awesome about your day today? Write or draw about it below:

S M T W TH F S Date __ / __ / __

I'm Thankful For:

1. _____

2. _____

3. _____

I was happy when I spent time with:

I feel:

What was awesome about your day today? Write or draw about it below:

S M T W TH F S Date __/__/__

I'm Thankful For:

1. _____
2. _____
3. _____

I was happy when I spent time with:

I feel:

What was awesome about your day today? Write or draw about it below:

S M T W TH F S Date __/__/__

I'm Thankful For:

1. _____

2. _____

3. _____

**I was happy when I
spent time with:**

I feel:

**What was awesome about your day today?
Write or draw about it below:**

S M T W TH F S Date __/__/__

I'm Thankful For:

1. _____

2. _____

3. _____

I was happy when I spent time with:

I feel:

What was awesome about your day today? Write or draw about it below:

I am Thankful for
My Friends

Write down the names of your
friends in the hearts below.

S M T W TH F S Date __/__/__

I'm Thankful For:

1. _____
2. _____
3. _____

I was happy when I spent time with:

I feel:

What was awesome about your day today? Write or draw about it below:

S M T W TH F S Date __/__/__

I'm Thankful For:

1. _____

2. _____

3. _____

I was happy when I spent time with:

I feel:

What was awesome about your day today?
Write or draw about it below:

S M T W TH F S Date __/__/__

I'm Thankful For:

1. _____
2. _____
3. _____

I was happy when I
spent time with:

I feel:

What was awesome about your day today?
Write or draw about it below:

S M T W TH F S Date __/__/__

I'm Thankful For:

1. _____

2. _____

3. _____

I was happy when I spent time with:

I feel:

What was awesome about your day today? Write or draw about it below:

S M T W TH F S Date __/__/__

I'm Thankful For:

1. _____

2. _____

3. _____

I was happy when I spent time with:

I feel:

What was awesome about your day today? Write or draw about it below:

I am grateful for Nature

Take a walk outside with your family and see what fun things you can find in nature!

S M T W TH F S Date __/__/__

I'm Thankful For:

1. _____

2. _____

3. _____

I was happy when I spent time with:

I feel:

What was awesome about your day today? Write or draw about it below:

S M T W TH F S Date __/__/__

I'm Thankful For:

1. _____
2. _____
3. _____

I was happy when I spent time with:

I feel:

What was awesome about your day today? Write or draw about it below:

S M T W TH F S Date __/__/__

I'm Thankful For:

1. _____

2. _____

3. _____

I was happy when I spent time with:

I feel:

What was awesome about your day today? Write or draw about it below:

S M T W TH F S Date __/__/__

I'm Thankful For:

1. _____

2. _____

3. _____

I was happy when I spent time with:

I feel:

What was awesome about your day today? Write or draw about it below:

S M T W TH F S Date __/__/__

I'm Thankful For:

1. _____

2. _____

3. _____

I was happy when I spent time with:

I feel:

What was awesome about your day today? Write or draw about it below:

www.ingramcontent.com/pod-product-compliance
Lightning Source LLC
Chambersburg PA
CBHW061221010425
24427CB00004B/42